Are you ready for an Art Attack?

This book is your ticket to the Art Attack circus, packed full of colourful ideas to bring the magic of the big top into your home. I'll show you how to create clowns, animals and circus folk with household junk and just a few craft essentials. Follow the easy steps and you'll be clowning around in no time!

So take your seats and get set for buckets of fun, let's have an Art Attack!

Contents

700029904904

Editor: Kate Tompsett
Designer: Charlotte Reilly
Artists: Mary Hall and Paul Gamble
Model Maker: Kate Tompsett

ROLL UP, ROLL UP!

This ringmaster will help hold your door open and welcome the audience in!

1 Fill a clean plastic bottle with sand or small pebbles and replace the lid. Cut a piece of card for the ringmaster's feet and glue it to the base of the bottle.

2 Using a mixture of PVA glue and water, paste kitchen paper to the bottom half of the bottle to pad out the ringmaster's legs. Scrunch up some more kitchen paper to give his feet a 3D look.

3 Glue a strip of card around the ringmaster's waist to make his cummerbund. Cut a jacket shape from card as shown and glue this around the bottle, too.

4 Fix pieces of rolled-up kitchen paper on with sticky tape to make the arms and lapels, then cover the whole thing with two layers of papier mâché. Roll up a ball of kitchen paper and tape it on top of the bottle to form his head.

5 Draw two circles on a piece of card, one inside the other, and cut them out to make the brim. The middle circle is the top of the hat. Wrap a rectangle of card around the circle and fix it on top of the brim with sticky tape. Put this on the ringmaster's head and cover it with a layer of papier maché.

6 When the papier maché is dry, paint the ringmaster. The traditional colours for his outfit are black and red, as shown here, but you could paint it any colour you like!

5

TOP THIS!

This big top storage box is great for keeping all your art materials neat and tidy!

Draw a triangle onto thick card. Draw a rectangle joining onto the triangle and cut out the whole shape. Draw around it five more times and cut out the shapes to give you six pieces.

YOU WILL NEED:

Thick card, red and yellow felt, PVA glue, newspaper, safety scissors, pencil, paints, paintbrush.

TURN THE TENT AROUND TO REVEAL A DIFFERENT ANIMAL!

2

Tape the shapes together as shown to make the tent, which will form the lid of your box. Cut a doorway in one of the sides.

3

Draw around the base of the tent onto cardboard and cut out a circle slightly smaller than the one you've just drawn. Wrap a strip of card around the circle and tape it into place. Cut two strips of card and make a slit in the middle of each one, then slot them together to make the dividers to go inside the box.

4

Cover the tent shape and the circular base with two layers of papier maché and leave them to dry.

5

Cover the tent with felt fabric. Glue strips of red and yellow felt around the sides, then add large triangles of felt to the roof of the tent.

6

Paint the outside of the box base white and the inside red and yellow. Draw and paint animals around the base. They will show through the door of the tent when you put the lid on.

WEIGHT & SEE!

1 Cut the flaps from a cardboard box. Tape a piece of card inside the box to make a shelf. Tape the long flaps from the box together to make the base.

2 Cut a strongman shape from card. Draw around it and cut it out again for strength. Cut two ovals of card to make his feet.

3 Partly blow up the balloons, so that one is larger than the other. Cover each balloon with three layers of torn-up newspaper and glue and leave them to dry.

4 Cut the largest balloon in half and fix one half to each side of the strongman's tummy. Do the same with the smaller balloon to form the head. Cover him with two layers of papier maché.

Fix the box to the strongman's hands, the feet to his ankles and the base to his feet. Use plenty of papier maché to fix it all together, paying special attention to the hands and feet. Leave it lying down for a few days to make sure it is completely dry.

5

YOU WILL NEED:
Cardboard, cardboard box, safety scissors, two balloons, PVA glue, sticky tape, newspaper, paints, paintbrush, gold star sequins.

6

Paint the strongman and the shelves. The leopard print design is easy — paint the strongman's outfit mustard yellow, then use a fine paintbrush to dab rings of black paint all over it.

CLOWNING AROUND!

THIS CRAZY CLOWN GAME WILL HAVE YOU LAUGHING ALL DAY!

1 Draw the outline of a clown onto card and cut it out. Draw around it and cut out a second clown.

2 Cut one of the clown shapes into sections and cover each piece with felt fabric.

3 Fix the felt-covered pieces onto the other cardboard clown shape.

4 Cut the eyes, nose and mouth from felt and add pieces of wool for hair. Put the scratchy part of the hook and loop dots onto the clown's hat, shoes, buttons and his nose.

Large piece of card, felt, cereal box card, wool, hook & loop sticky dots, PVA glue, safety scissors, pencil.

PERFECT POM-POMS!

Cut two doughnut shapes from card. Place them together and cut a long piece of wool. Start to wrap it around the card pieces, by pushing the wool through the hole.

Keep wrapping lengths of wool around the doughnut shape, until the hole in the centre has filled up.

Carefully cut along the edges of the circle, pushing the scissors between the two pieces of card. Ask an adult to help if this is tricky.

When you've cut all the way around the edge, cut another piece of wool and thread it between the two circles of card. Tie it into a tight knot. Now you can pull the cardboard rings off! Stick the soft part of the hook and loop dots onto the pom-poms.

AIM THE POM-POMS AT THE CLOWN TO FINISH HIS OUTFIT!

GRRRR-EAT!

MAKE YOUR OWN MOVING CIRCUS SCENE!

1 Trace or photocopy the pictures on the opposite page and stick them onto thin card. Colour in all the pieces.

2 Carefully cut out all the pictures, following the dotted lines. Make holes where marked at A, B, C and D.

3 Attach the lion and lion tamer to the background using paper fasteners. Match up the letters to make sure that you are putting the pieces in the right places.

FANCY THAT!

SILLY SHOES!

WITH THIS COOL COSTUME, YOU'LL BE THE BEST-DRESSED CLOWN IN TOWN!

1 Cut a large shoe shape from thick card.

2 Tape two pieces of corrugated card to one side of the shoe. Bend them over into arch shapes and tape them to the other side of the shoe shape.

3 Cut slits at each end of the arched pieces of card, bend down the flaps you've made and tape them down.

4 Cut a hole in the shoe that is big enough to take your foot. Cut two more slits in the top of the shoe to form the tongue. Make holes as shown for the laces to go through – ask an adult to help with this. Repeat these steps to make a second shoe, making sure it fits the other foot!

5 Cover the shoes with two layers of papier maché and leave them to dry.

6 Paint the shoes with bright colours. When they are dry, thread a piece of cord through the holes and tie it in a bow.

Cardboard, bendy card, safety scissors, small balloon, PVA glue, sticky tape, newspaper, paints, paintbrush, pom-poms, fun fur, wool, cord, elastic, felt fabric, safety pin.

TO MAKE THE NOSE, COVER A SMALL BALLOON IN PAPIER MACHÉ, PAINT IT RED, THEN MAKE 2 HOLES AND THREAD A PIECE OF ELASTIC THROUGH.

CUT TWO FLOWER SHAPES FROM DIFFERENT COLOURED FELT, STICK THEM TOGETHER THEN ADD A SAFETY PIN AT THE BACK.

HILARIOUS HAT!

1 Cut a large circle of thin card. Cut a section from it that is just over a quarter of the circle. Roll it up and use sticky tape to fix it in a cone shape.

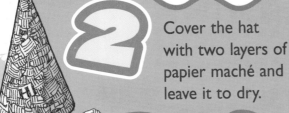

2 Cover the hat with two layers of papier maché and leave it to dry.

3 Paint the hat with your favourite colour and leave it to dry.

4 Glue a strip of fun fur around the base of the hat and stick on three pom-poms. Glue lengths of wool inside the rim of the hat to make groovy clown hair. Don't worry about the length of each piece of wool – you can always give it a haircut later!

15

SADDLE UP!

THIS CLIP-CLOP CLIPBOARD IS SURE TO IMPRESS YOUR FRIENDS AND NEIGH-BOURS!

1

Copy this horse shape onto a sheet of card. Cut it out and draw around it again. Glue the pieces together for strength.

2

Paint the horse light grey with darker grey details and a black outline. Leave it to dry.

3

Cut lots of pieces of wool for the mane. Put a line of glue along the horse's neck and lay the wool over it. Fold the ends over the back of the horse and tape them down. Use sticky tape to add lengths of wool to the horse's bottom! This forms his tail.

YOU WILL NEED:

Large pieces of thick card, pencil, scissors, grey wool, paints, paintbrush, sequins, stick-on gems, pairs of magnets, PVA glue, sticky tape, feathers, felt.

4

Cut a saddle from card, plus two pieces of card for his headdress. Cover them with felt fabric and decorate them with sequins. Glue the headdress onto the horse, with the feathers tucked behind it.

5

You need to use magnets in pairs. Glue one magnet to the saddle, and the one that goes with it to a gemstone. Repeat with as many gems and magnets as you like.

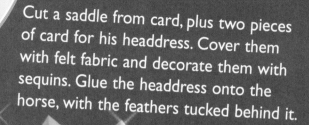

ART ATTACK

Dear Katie
Thank you for my birthday present and for being my best friend!
Love from
Laura
x x x x

HELLO!

6

Glue the saddle to the horse. Apply glue only to the middle of the saddle so that you can tuck important notes behind it.

IN THE RING!

MAKE THIS MINI CIRCUS RING AND FIND OUT WHERE THE REAL CIRCUS ACTION HAPPENS!

YOU WILL NEED:

Thick card, small cardboard box, safety scissors, pencil, sticky tape, newspaper, PVA glue, paints, paintbrush, sand, lolly sticks, modelling clay, drinking straws, sweet tube, two yoghurt pots, tin foil.

CIRCUS RING

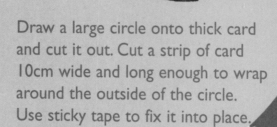

1

Draw a large circle onto thick card and cut it out. Cut a strip of card 10cm wide and long enough to wrap around the outside of the circle. Use sticky tape to fix it into place.

3

Paint the box white on the inside and blue on the outside. Decorate the outside edge with yellow stars – you can use paint or stick on shapes cut from craft foam. Spread glue over the bottom of the box and pour sand over the glue.

2 Cover the box with a layer of torn-up newspaper and glue and leave it to dry.

BALLS

The balls are made with modelling clay. Roll one red and one yellow ball the same size. Cut each of them into quarters, then fix the quarters back together as shown.

UNICYCLE

The unicycle is made from thin strips of card. Glue a strip of card into a ring and add tiny pieces of card for spokes, a strip of card for the post and an oval of card for the saddle. Leave it to dry, then paint it.

CAGE

The tiger's cage is made with lolly sticks glued together and painted black.

CANNON

Paint a sweet tube black and glue it to two black pieces of card so it stands up.

DIVING BOARD

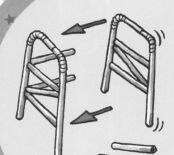

The diving board frame is made from drinking straws. Push two straws into each other to make one side of the frame and add short pieces of straw between them for strength. Make another one the same. When they are dry, fix them together with more short pieces of straw.

Make a small house with a slanted roof from cardboard and glue it to the top of the straws. Leave it to dry overnight, then paint it.

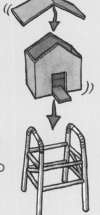

Paint a jelly pot and stuff it with card or paper, then add a disc of tin foil on top to look like water.

BRING ON THE CLOWNS!

CREATE THIS MADCAP CIRCUS SCENE AND WATCH THE CROWD GO WILD!

Make the base of the circus ring from a piece of yellow craft foam. Cut a squashed circle shape and stick it onto a piece of thin, dark-coloured card.

Surround the circle of foam with strips of corrugated paper. Make it wider at the front of the picture so it looks closer and decorate it with shiny stars.

Cut the clown's car from a piece of multicoloured paper, you could use wrapping paper. Use silver card for the bumpers and cut out circles from a black bin liner for the wheels.

The people in the audience are made from scraps of felt. Cut lots of different hairstyles and draw faces on with a marker pen. Stick them onto the background in rows.

Each clown is made with scraps of different coloured paper. Wrapping paper is perfect for bright clown clothes! Glue googly eyes in place and stick on short pieces of wool for hair.

The ball and pedestal are made from coloured paper, covered with sequin waste. This is the part that's left over when sequins are made, you can find it in most craft shops.

Stick on some sequins to look like coloured confetti coming out of this clown's bucket!

SIGNED AND SEALED!

GIVE YOUR ROOM THE ART ATTACK SEAL OF APPROVAL!

1 Put the flour and salt into a bowl, and slowly mix in the water. Squish the dough between your hands until it feels smooth and stretchy.

2 Sprinkle some flour over your work surface and roll out the dough. Cut a rectangle to form the base.

3 Draw a seal, a star, a circle and a pedestal onto paper and cut out the individual pieces to use as templates.

4 Roll out the dough again. Lay the templates onto the dough and ask an adult to help you cut around them with the rounded knife. Place them on the rectangular base.

5 You can leave the dough to dry for a day or two, or ask an adult to cook it in the oven at 180°C, 350°F, gas mark 4 for about half an hour.

6 When the dough is dry (or cool if you cooked it), paint it in bright, contrasting colours.

7 Add details with black paint and a fine paintbrush. Write your name in pencil first, then go over it with black paint. Finish with a layer of PVA glue to make it nice and shiny.

PAINT YOUR SIGN IN BOLD COLOURS SO IT REALLY STANDS OUT!

HOOP HOOP

1 Draw a picture of a clown onto card and cut it out. Make sure there's an arch between his feet. Draw around the shape again, cut it out and glue the shapes together for strength.

2 Cut two semi-circles of card, each one with a slot in the top. Cut slots in each of the clown's feet and fix the semi-circles of card onto them. Your clown should now stand up!

3 Use sticky tape to fix the drinking chocolate tub onto the cardboard tube to make a mallet. Cover it with torn-up newspaper and glue and leave it to dry.

4 Paint the clown and the mallet in bright, wacky colours!

24

HOORAY!

YOU WILL NEED:

Pencil, large piece of card, safety scissors, newspaper, PVA glue, sticky tape, paints, paintbrush, long cardboard tube, drinking chocolate tub, balloons, rice, clingfilm.

5

To make the ball, wrap some rice in a piece of clingfilm. Cut the neck off a balloon and stretch the balloon over the ball of rice. Keep adding more balloons until you can no longer see the rice.

MAKE AS MANY CLOWNS AS YOU LIKE. THIS ONE IS DOING A HANDSTAND!

PARTY TIME!

YOU WILL NEED:
Potato, craft foam, string, elastic band, coloured card, paint.

CREATE YOUR OWN PERSONALISED PARTY INVITATIONS!

Use the edge of a piece of craft foam to print the words. Bend it round to make the curved letters.

Cut balloon shapes from craft foam and use the edge of a long piece of craft foam to print the strings.

Cut a horse shape from card and print it in brown paint. Use string dipped in darker brown paint to print his tail and mane.

To make the acrobat, ask an adult to help you cut a potato in half and carve out the different shapes. Dip each piece in some paint and press it onto the paper, then add the details with a fine paintbrush or a marker pen.

The zigzag pattern at the top and bottom are printed with a short piece of elastic band. Glue it to the end of a piece of card to use as a handle. Use your fingertip to print the dots.

HOW ABOUT MAKING UP SOME DIFFERENT DESIGNS? YOU COULD PRINT A CLOWN'S FACE OR SOME CIRCUS ANIMALS!